Sergey Biryukov

TRANSFORMATIONS

Translated from the Russian
by Erina Megowan and Anatoly Kudryavitsky

SurVision Books

First published in 2018 by
SurVision Books
Dublin, Ireland
www.survisionmagazine.com

Copyright © Sergey Biryukov, 2018
Translations © Erina Megowan, 2018
Translations © Anatoly Kudryavitsky, 2018

Cover image © Anatoly Kudryavitsky, 2018

Design © SurVision Books, 2018

ISBN: 978-1-9995903-5-2

This book is in copyright. No part of this publication may be reproduced, stored in a retrieval system or transmitted in any form or by any means without the prior permission in writing from the publisher.

Acknowledgements

Grateful acknowledgement is made to the editors of the following, in which a number of these poems originally appeared:

Poetry Ireland Review, SurVision, Drugoe Polusharie, A Night in the Nabokov Hotel: 20 Contemporary Russian Poets anthology (Dedalus Press, Ireland, 2006), *Mirror Sand: An Anthology of Russian Short Poems* (Glagoslav Publications, UK, 2018.)

CONTENTS

Underwater Poems   3
The End of August   9
"Fleeing wind of morning..."   10
"But not..."   11
"Po-..."   12
Yet Another   13
"Lighting one cigarette..."   14
"As If Resolved..."   15
Most Concise Definition of a Philosopher   16
Sphinx   17
Toward a Portrait of John Cage   18
Beastmen   19
The Treble Clef   20
News of Petrarch and Laura   21
Everything Changes   22
Who's Good   23
In Magritte's House   24
Toward a Sign   25
Universum   26
The Golem in Prague   28
Toward Faust   30
A Dream Continued   31

Pages 4 to 18 translated by Erina Megowan.
Pages 19 to 31 translated by Anatoly Kudryavitsky.

Underwater Poems

*

To swim under water
to touch the fins
of flowing fish
and listen to
the dumb language
to see
the movements
of lips
Why sorrow

*

Stone under water
water's stone
you're here
you're there
shadow slippery
only
shadow
shadow
doh

*

Under water
can't say
A
Water pours
into the mouth
flips you
over
back to front
You don't know
what's better
being there
or here
You're dull
you're foolish
here
But there?
A?

*

Try to run
on sharp pebbles
on Anapa's beach
Where where
is a thread
which Parcae weaves
Where is the essence
of waves
of raves
We're free to
acknowledge mother
Myth
of
pa
in

*

Salt is salt
motif
and quivering
of grass
Be firm
be right
Oh what is there
still
is there
still
on the day's
horizon
The rays of sun
rising
rising
from the sea

*

No signs exist
of that
that you
still can live
you drowned twice
but you were saved
thank you
for what
sorry

*

Loneliness
to cherish
to walk off
when
all are right
but you – left
that is, not
right
and laughter
of veins

*

Difficult, it turns out
to write poems
underneath water
Even on sand
they slip away
not remaining
not one line
think, not one
underneath water
if you can
sing
howl

The End of August

In the last days of August
on the eve of school
you remember
the white shirt
the red tie
given by brother
the scent of apples in the briefcase
the whiteness of a notebook sheet
the cages for ciphers
the lines for letters
the read in the summer textbooks
the expeditions to distant countries
on the geographical atlas
the comprehension of physics' laws
in the cold river
the smell of baked potatoes
the smoke of a bonfire
the Moscow girl
who came for vacation
Who said they study anatomy
in the 10th grade?
Ah, really!
End of August
song "Autumn on the threshold
August behind the windows"
How does it continue
in this incredible play...

***

Fleeing wind of morning
To wake up astonished

Here is darkness

Green mills' crosses
fog of village outskirts

Audible
the crunch of an apple

Return

possible

***

But not

That does
resemble denial

if denial
could
deny itself

if it were like that
it were

and in us
ourselves
exists

but not

***

Po-
etry
is an
off-
ense
not subject to
ex-
posure

***

As if resolved is
the equation of the sun

What is wind for
and rain with snow

and desert frost

and a cloud of vapor

God knows the remaining

Yet Another

Yet another summer
departed bird-like
track – it's a pair of scars
on the heart
cross resembling
optical sight of a rifle
there really are exact shooters

***

Lighting one cigarette
from another's tip
inhaling
observing how blazes up in darkness
a fiery-red light
grinding pebbles
of yesterday
as instantly
as a flash of magnesium
as a Latin saying

Most Concise Definition of a Philosopher

Philosopher – it is a person, who doesn't fear being a
                                                                               philosopher.
Philosopher – it is a person, who doesn't fear being a person.
Philosopher – it is a person, who doesn't fear being.
Philosopher – it is a person, who doesn't fear.
Philosopher – it is a person, who doesn't.
Philosopher – it is a person, who.
Philosopher – it is a person.
Philosopher it is!
Philosopher!

(Read distinctly, gradually strengthening the voice. Repeat everything in the opposite order.)
Philosopher!
Philosopher it is!
Philosopher – it is a person.
Philosopher – it is a person, who.
Philosopher – it is a person, who doesn't.
Philosopher – it is a person, who doesn't fear.
Philosopher – it is a person, who doesn't fear being.
Philosopher – it is a person, who doesn't fear being a person.
Philosopher – it is a person, who doesn't fear being a
                                                                               philosopher.

Sphinx

Taciturn sphinx
at the maritime gates
of St. Petersburg
you meet sailors
with silence

you listen attentively to
their conversations
about distant countries
you memorise things
like a computer
and then will retell
descendants
likewise silently

stillness does not frighten you
and rush of waves
and mysterious
quiver of silken cloth
on hips of a girl
who came out towards
one returning from sail

he will tell you
"hello sphinx"
and you likewise silently
will answer him with a greeting
and then he will understand
that he's back home

Toward a Portrait of John Cage

At John Cage
I looked
he was old
from the year 12
(thousand nine hundred)
and laughed
without sound
like a pterodactyl
he said something
but not that clearly
chain of circumstance
permanent
anarchy is the mother of order

Beastmen

In the same old way
you get out of your beds
of your graves
—beastmen—
gather some food
rodents
vegetables
and take it all
back to your crypts

Inscriptions: signboards...
the genuine ones
dissolved in space
or in time
no tombstones
on their graves
none whatsoever

The Treble Clef

One hand is held up by the other
over the note A
of a high octave.
What glory has achieved,
cannot be tamed.
Those were the days of the Chief
Difficulties and the all-out search for fame.
Can you possibly imagine
people as complex as metallic alloys?
Their black magic, their unchanging habit
of embittering a man by trying his patience.
What breaks the seal of silence
is the treble clef, not a picklock.

News of Petrarch and Laura

Laura types a letter to Petrarch
in the Times New Roman font
it's her blog

and it disappears

Petrarch types a sonnet for Laura
his fingers run along the keyboard

the sonnet disappears

the petals of syllables
fall onto Laura's frock

silence lingers
the two of them sit so close
he'd touch her little finger
should he stretch his right hand
into Cyberland

Everything Changes

Everything changes
Heraclitus was right
or what was his name
never mind
everything changes me...
and a bell
tolls
for somebody
a paper bell

Who's Good?

Shadows
the rustling of shadows
and no good man
wears blinkers in the shade
who's good
goody-goofy-good?
Richard Roe, John Doe –
neither that shadow
nor the next

In Magritte's House

For Philip Meersman

The snail sank into Olympia's womb
eternity and impossibility
transpersonality
but
the curl of Georgette's pain
René Magritte writes in the kitchen
the coffee boils
the pipe whizzes
the faceless man
impersonates a wardrobe
The world of things
its effortless reincarnation
A few more seconds –
and the street
will dash
after it

Toward a Sign

For Jerzy Faryno

To find out about the roots of trees
how they move backward
toward a sign
toward the square root of minus one
to comprehend that backward movement
this is what I call
an insight
at the sign level, at the meta level
and a movement
from some spot to another
and back
is the reverse of a sign
(something to remember)

Universum

and so
   away you go
on the steamer of time
      to comprehend Universum
lightly dressed
    in case
you suffer a shipwreck
      and swim across the ocean
of doubts
     on a helpful
cloud
      not understanding yet
that you already are
     inside
Universum
      which engulfs you
on all sides

you thump
      against the corners of time
against its figured
    numbers
(sometimes prickly
sometimes imperceptibly smooth)
and you still think that Universum
     is somewhere there
some distance away
      and the compass needle

is pointing in its direction
      or an arrow on the map
of Treasure Island

      the language of an unknown tribe
   is revealed to you
  you begin to understand
the "fleeting" talk:
universum-universum-universum

   on all sides

The Golem in Prague

They say, some fragments of the Golem
are kept in the attic of an old
Prague synagogue

all of a sudden the pieces
stick together
form the Golem's torso –

and out he goes
for a night stroll
in spicy Prague

along Surrealism Quay
up Poetism Prospect
down Nezval Street
and Teige Road

he tries to jump over
Kafka Square
with its
jackdaws and crows

the Golem walks naked
leaving no trace

goes unspotted
leaps

or makes divisible
movements

tunnels
between
night and day

Toward Faust

They give away half the kingdom
having marked it with some prattle
their legs interlaced
over the river
so that's what it is
your life
won't begin anew
hence
"Beautiful moment,
do not pass away!"

a passer-by says
bitte could you show me the way to Faust?
wie lange dauert
this commotion?

I once passed here
casually
without looking
at the erased houses

but now what
but where do we go from here
but on we go

A Dream Continued

It's impossible to remember but still
—at least in scraps—
you can memorise the continuation
of a dream
some unknown place
looking like a classroom
bags and backpacks dumped
all over the floor
a few familiar faces
though inaccurately outlined
is he really or does he only resemble
is she or isn't she
as if you've returned from Goodness knows
where or she's come back from nothingness
a conversation
full of omissions and ambiguities
glowing cigarettes the clicks of lighters
the reverse sequence of events
you answer a predicted question
scratch your nose
having learned the news
actually words are missing too
only half-words are left
fragments of speech
devastation
a continuation of a dream
a semblance of infini...

More poetry published by SurVision Books
in our New Poetics Series:

Noelle Kocot. Humanity
   (New Poetics: USA)
   ISBN 978-1-9995903-0-7

Ciaran O'Driscoll. The Speaking Trees
   (New Poetics: Ireland)
   ISBN 978-1-9995903-1-4

Elin O'Hara Slavick. Cameramouth
   (New Poetics: USA)
   ISBN 978-1-9995903-4-5

Anatoly Kudryavitsky. Stowaway
   (New Poetics: Ireland)
   ISBN 978-1-9995903-2-1

Sergey Biryukov. Transformations
   Translated from Russian
   (New Poetics: Russia)
   ISBN 978-1-9995903-5-2

Our books are available to order via
http://survisionmagazine.com/books.htm

www.ingramcontent.com/pod-product-compliance
Lightning Source LLC
Chambersburg PA
CBHW061315040426
42444CB00010B/2657